MW01171623

10 Little Rules
When Good Jobs Go Bad

Learn, Grow and Reclaim Your Power ...
at Work and in Life

by
Kathleen Goggin

ISBN: 979-8-9901971-8-3

Published by Little Rules Publishing

Other books in the 10 Little Rules Series

10 Little Rules for a Blissy Life
by Carol Pearson

10 Little Rules for Your Creative Soul
by Rita Long

10 Little Rules of Hank
by Wendy Price

10 Little Rules for Finding Your Truth
by Micki Beach

10 Little Rules for Mermaids
by Amy Hege Atwell

10 Little Rules for the Modern Southern Belle
by Beverly Ingle

10 Little Rules for Serving You
by Amy Hege Atwell

10 Little Rules for Sharing Your Story
by Frank Winters

www.10littlerules.com

DEDICATION

To my family, for everything.

Kathleen Goggin

ACKNOWLEDGMENTS

I want to thank:

The Loudoun County (VA) Rust Library Writers' Group and the Roanoke (VA) Regional Writers' Group for their superior support and solidarity.

The "hive" writers' group for their daily inspiration and reliable reality check.

Natalya Pestalozzi, PCC, MAPP, for your powerful perspective and feedback.

Kathleen Goggin

DISCLAIMER

This book depicts actual events and people and reflects my personal recollections over time. Some individuals' names and identifying traits have been changed to protect their privacy, some dialogue has been edited for brevity, and some event timelines have been compressed.

My work is based on my recollections, coworker interviews, and online research. This work is published for general reference, and I do not provide any legal, financial, or psychological advice. I hereby waive any personal liability, either directly or indirectly, for the advice or information presented within.

Kathleen Goggin

FOREWORD

This book came about in the most beautifully organic way ... through a new and growing friendship, shared professional respect, and deep conversations about work, life, hopes, dreams ... and how easily they can get derailed.

This is the book I wish I had read at the beginning of my career. I am incredibly grateful for the opportunities I've had and where they've led me, yet there were so many times I felt helpless, out of control and ... lost.

Kate has created something powerful. It's been magical working with her to bring this into the world.

Carol Pearson
Founder & Publisher

Kathleen Goggin

CONTENTS

Kathleen Goggin

INTRODUCTION

I've been thinking a lot about career choices lately — how each decision shapes who we are, what we do, and how we live our lives. Was there a plan, and did it all add up to satisfaction in the end? Or was it a journey of self-discovery through a lot of trial and error? Or maybe a little bit of both?

This book tackles those questions and shares my path through the job maze. I have been fortunate to work in unique roles in the United States and overseas with incredibly talented people. I learned so much, and I valued my time with them.

It wasn't easy though, and I faced one difficult career decision after another.

I was a latch-key kid who grew up absorbing women's liberation chants. They said I could have it all — job, family and financial success — I just wish they had explained how tough it is to have it all at the same time.

So often, I was filled with self-doubt, following the rules I had read from the latest Harvard Business Review or online post. Was I creating my brand correctly, networking daily, promotion-ready, and quietly quitting, while believing I could be a successful working mom? That is the dream the Web suggests; the problem is those rules never fit well with my reality.

I had to accept that sometimes I was relieved to do what I was told. I wasn't responsible for the outcome if I followed someone else's rules. While there was some temporary comfort in those situations, it meant I was avoiding self-direction and determination in the long run.

Additionally, I was generally convinced there was a straight line to success. I learned over and over again it seemed more like Dorothy's winding yellow brick road trip toward Oz. I wondered if I was searching for an ideal job instead of realizing my personal power to change course at any time.

I naively grappled with outdated concepts such as waiting for a fair system of hard work and reward, and assuming management knows what they are doing.

Along the way, I met legions of people with the same questions. Young and old, male and female, they wanted to hear the truth from me, someone who had been there and done that. They were facing their own difficult decisions, especially when they did everything right, yet nothing worked.

"My boss hates me, and he's trying to fire me," my colleague would say, "I can't quit. What should I do?" Or "I took over for the manager four months ago, but my company won't give me the promotion salary. Should I stick it out or leave?" Or "I'm bored silly and losing my mind; what can I do while I wait to leave? And "My coworker is psychotic, the boss doesn't care, how can I fix this?"

I heard a lot of self-doubt and self-blaming. My co-worker, eyes cast to the floor, would say, "I did all the research. I asked all the right questions, yet I feel like I made a big mistake taking this job. I can't afford to quit; what can I do now?"

I totally understood and shared my similar experiences and strategies. A dream job to one person is a bad job to another. It's all subjective and depends on your personality, work history, and life phase.

I started working at age 15 and had the usual progression of jobs — babysitting for neighbors, cutting lawns, and working in retail. Like most people, I grew up through work, which was not always a graceful maturation process.

The job cycle is as follows: you hear about a job, go through the recruitment process, get hired and oriented, work for the organization, and then leave or offboard.

You take every job assuming it is a good one, yet at any point, you may get an intuition that something has changed. It could be the organization or you. Either way though, only you can fix your work and your life.

In my case, I had to learn this lesson over and over again, the hard way.

Bad bosses or companies, work/life balance issues, toxic cultures, boredom, and unrealistic expectations — all are reasons why good jobs go bad — wrecking your emotional, professional, and financial life, sometimes simultaneously.

I frequently make lemonade out of rotten lemons, reacting to one environment after another without much control. I needed my own rules to make sense of it all and to change my behavior. I also had to come to terms with my stories and honestly ask myself if and how I had contributed to a good job going bad.

It took my whole career to find the courage, commitment, and community to finally feel more self-directed and satisfied.

According to recent research, we spend one-third of our lives working (Pryce-Jones, 2010), yet I suspect it's even longer for most of us. That's all the more reason to optimize our potential for happiness at work.

While my career pivoted to accommodate a family, careers can pivot for various reasons — including starting or finishing a relationship, responding to financial emergencies and opportunities, or pursuing passion projects and travel.

I'm no job coach. I'm your coworker, neighbor, or auntie, and I hear you. I hope these stories help you discuss your crazy career ride and feel less alone. This is the book I wish I had when I started more than 30 years ago.

I dedicate it to anyone trying to find their way. I hope my rules save you heartaches and headaches on your journey.

Kathleen Goggin

RULE 1
Know Your "Now or Never" Moment

Good jobs go bad for many reasons. Sometimes, it's a mismatch between your career goal and the job opportunity. When this happens, the unrealistic expectations that grow in that gap can be intense — so intense that you might find yourself in what I call a "now or never" moment.

My job producing news conferences at the National Press Club (NPC) was one of those. I witnessed history daily, worked with the world's best journalists, and my office was located next to the bar. My friends and family marveled at who I met, and they wanted to know every behind-the-scenes story. Was Neil Armstrong short? Patrick Stewart handsome? Ted Kennedy smart?

Who could complain? I could. I was asking myself every day — you got what you wanted; you love this organization; what is this nagging sense that you made a misstep taking this job?

When I applied for the job, I hoped it would be a stepping stone to a writing career. At the time, I was returning from Western Europe where our family had supported my husband's government job. Though I wanted to pursue freelance writing then, like many military and government "trailing spouses" I felt pressure to choose a more secure job instead. I still harbored a goal of full-time writing someday and I welcomed a job near journalists. I believed it would open doors for me.

The NPC leaders appreciated my event management skills, yet my interest in watching history unfold soon faded. I dragged into the office after a long commute, and the job's stress had prevented us from getting pregnant.

Then in the spring, I reached my breaking point. During that week, I scrambled to cover four high-profile events, one each day. The line-up was Canadian Prime Minister Jean Chretien, author Stephen Ambrose, entertainer Whoopi Goldberg, and South Korean Presidential candidate Kim De-Jung. Each event sold out.

I was the point person for each speaker and their entourage. That meant I was the one who met 10

Canadian Embassy staff members assisting Prime Minister Chretien. I greeted the group as they stepped off the mahogany elevator.

"We need to meet with your protocol liaison."

That would be me.

"Your event organizer, producer, day-of facilitator."

Me. Me. Me.

I began the walk-and-talk tour, discussing the schedule while answering pop-up questions and noting issues. It's not that I was anything special; it's that I had no support staff, and every NPC president is a working journalist who volunteers their time for the year-long appointment. I was it.

The scenario played out again with the folks from the Ambrose staff and the South Korean embassy. For the Goldberg lunch, there were even more unique challenges. Over the previous weeks, Ms. Goldberg had requested that the NPC reserve special travel accommodations to the event. I drafted the president's negative replies, as the NPC does not pay for speaker expenses at newsmaker luncheon events. Although she arrived in good humor and delivered a fantastic speech about celebrity press coverage, I know the situation caused Ms. Goldberg some irritation, and that increased my stress.

It was a long week, and by the time of the De-Jung event on Friday, I found myself sitting on the worn steps of the press gallery, half-listening to him in an exhausted stupor. My mind was struggling to recall why I applied for this job and how this incredible opportunity had quickly become rote and routine.

I made my way back to my office, where a young journalist stopped in and asked, "Who's coming next week?"

I took this in slowly. My mouth opened, yet nothing came out. I thought about all the worry I had endured this week, how everything had gone seamlessly, how no one cared about that, and how this work seemed so empty now.

I wrung my hands, careful to hide my emotions from this perfectly nice man who was just part of the media machine that needed feeding. I could immediately see I no longer wanted to be part of it. I was done.

My mind raced, and I thought, "Okay, how do I fix this? Can I fix this? Where would I go, and what would I do? What will people say? Am I sabotaging my career?"

I drove home that night, mulling over my confused motivations for the job. I was so wrong to think "getting a foot in the door" would succeed. It might have worked for my mom's generation, but not mine. And where was my writing plan? I did not want to be a Washington, D.C.

journalist grinding out the daily news. I immersed myself in blame.

It was probably divine intervention that led me to Julia Cameron and her book, "The Artist's Way: A Spiritual Path to Higher Creativity." I started journaling for her "morning pages" exercise; soon, my reflections became a vital reality check.

I noted the nonsense of my daily life, and sometimes a pearl would pop up, like "Own your day before someone else does." The more I journaled, the more I questioned myself about my real desires. I learned the critical ones were: What do I want? What am I willing to do to get it? What am I willing to sacrifice?

Aha! It was that last bit that I was skipping. I was so focused on the wanting and the planning that I never truly understood that every change comes at a price, and it's important to consider it upfront.

Journaling helped me be honest with myself. It reinforced what I heard author Alice Walker once say: "If you want to know how you got to where you are today, look back six months in your journal."

I decided this was my "now-or-never moment" to quit my job and work part-time. Doing so would allow me to decrease the stress, continue thoughtfully writing, and hopefully grow our family. My husband was supportive, and we agreed to accept the financial risk.

I gladly turned over my office keys to Leigh Ann, a caring colleague who was ready to take over my job and start her new journey.

Yet many people, including some other co-workers, did not understand or agree with my decision. I realized this was the sting I was avoiding — public perception and reputation. I had to release that. I was too dependent on the view of others, especially from people who did not know my real goals or dreams.

Slowing down and confronting my true motivations paid off. Within two months of leaving the NPC, I was pregnant with our second child.   ·

I soaked up that peaceful time and thrived creatively. Freelance writing was the perfect setup for staying home with my baby and working on passion projects.

I updated a nonfiction book to help new immigrants adjust to the United States and self-published an online newsletter for people moving abroad.

Titled *The Art of International Living*, it was a critical success and featured in The Washington Post. It helped diverse groups navigate the ups and downs of overseas life, and I savored this meaningful work.

I would return to this theme of "writing for good," as Julia Cameron calls it (Cameron, 2002), many times throughout of my career. Not only did her journaling lessons help me identify my now or never moment, but her writing advice influenced many of my later decisions to support critical programs for the public good.

Kathleen Goggin

your turn...

Know your "now or never" moment

To uncover your true motivations, try journaling each day. Mornings work best for me, but find your rhythm. I write stream-of-consciousness, and I get to the meaty stuff after about five minutes. I don't go back and read it right away. I let it simmer, usually about a week. When I do go back to review, I am amazed at how I repeatedly discover some new wisdom, confront my babbling bullshit, and find clarity.

For example, I recently scanned all entries from the last six months and noted what I wanted and how many times I mentioned it. I circled the recurring items. It reinforced my evolving feelings and goals. This continual writing, reflecting, and reviewing process has helped me identify perceived obstacles and creative solutions.

Now, it's your turn. On the next few pages, write your answers to these questions:

When will you know the cost is too high to continue as is? How much energy do you expend pretending to care?

What do you want, what are you willing to do to get it, and what are you willing to sacrifice?

Dig deep and be honest with yourself. Is this your now-or-never moment?

RULE 2
Claim Your Power

After several years in another overseas tour to support my husband's career, I returned to the United States again. I also found myself toe-to-toe with the devil.

We returned this time from Eastern Europe, where I had produced an embassy newsletter. With two valuable letters of recommendation from two Ambassadors in my pocket, I was ready to reenter the job market.

Based on an NPC member's referral, I secured a D.C. job. We faced a pricey housing market, and I was incredibly grateful to have a position lined up so our combined salaries could qualify us for a mortgage.

Days after returning, we were in a Northern Virginia hotel with a rental car. My husband, now 7-year-old son, and I were focused on our long to-do list: start new jobs, buy a house, register for school.

We were excited to be home, yet my husband was not well. He had a whirlwind departure from his post with a dozen meetings and field visits, so it was no surprise that he was quite pale and exhausted with zero energy.

On the other hand, our son was rested and ready to explore, visit relatives, and speak English to everyone in the grocery store line. His enthusiasm helped us overcome our jet lag.

It was the day before July 4th, and my husband was determined to go to his new office as scheduled for an initial check-in and orientation. After dropping him at the subway, I started our house hunt. My new job would start a week later.

Midday, my cell rang.

"I don't feel well; you need to come get me," my husband said, no small talk and very urgent. He blurted out a location and said, "Come now." My husband is usually a very easy-going guy, so I knew something was off. I immediately headed downtown with my son in the back seat.

When I pulled over, I found him pacing on the sidewalk, holding his head. He got in, cringing in the front passenger seat, and said, "My head hurts. I feel dizzy. I need to lay down."

I was even more worried when we got "home" to the hotel. He tried to get out of the car but could not walk straight. He gripped the car frame and reached for the brick wall, feeling his way to the hotel door.

"I need to get you to the hospital," I said, while his irritation grew louder. "No, I need to lay down; get me to the room."

He collapsed in the bed, cradling his head. No regular meds helped, and he asked me to turn off the lights and leave him alone. "Okay, it's a migraine from the jet lag and the re-entry stress," I thought. I gave up on my emergency room request and let him rest.

I slept in the other room and hoped he would be well enough to celebrate the July 4th holiday. In the morning, my son and I were ready for fun. I peeked in to check on my husband and seeing him ghastly pale, I knew the holiday would be very different. I ignored his resistance to the ER, and we headed straight there.

They poked and prodded and made him walk down the hall. Still sideways, he grabbed the handrails, moving slowly.

We told them that a few weeks ago, while overseas, he had a tooth extracted, and it left a big hole in his mouth with a subsequent infection. The burly doctor grunted, "That explains it. Now it's turned into a brain infection."

His words swept over us as we acknowledged the antibiotics and pain meds and instructions to follow up with a neurologist.

This health crisis quickly became a life-changing event for us both, leaving my husband with debilitating pain — headache, dizziness, ear ringing, hearing loss — and, most significantly, short-term memory loss.

He used sick leave to delay his job restart, and I settled into a new routine of his care amid house-hunting and my job preparations. I was overwhelmed and flat-out scared. I had no choice but to bear down on my to-do list, hoping he would heal, and everything would work out.

I started my new communications job part-time, with the understanding that it would be full-time in a few weeks after we ironed out our housing and resettled.

The boss was a former network news anchor who had come to D.C. as a public relations staffer for her US senator. After her Capitol Hill experience, she landed at this small agency, as a communication director. Like other journalists, she missed the newsroom urgency and tried to recreate it with her staff daily. Barking orders, demanding unreasonable deadlines, and publicly denigrating workers were not a formula for success in a small, slow-paced agency.

My first impression was that she seemed outwardly nice, although her short temper and impatience were notable under the surface. She always appeared to be waiting for a live shot that never came.

I was one of two public affairs specialists on a small team that also included an editor and a graphic designer.

Every day I went home exhausted but ready to care for my husband and son and do house-hunting chores.

My realtor queued up houses during the week. Then, on weekend mornings, we would bring my husband to look at two or three houses before he lost energy and returned to bed. He was not improving, and my worry was constant.

We found a neat Cape Cod near my son's school. The location was perfect, but the house needed a TON of work. During the walkthrough, my husband sat on the screened-in back porch and was reminded of his childhood home. Those memories flooded his face as he glanced from the porch to the lush green yard. I thought, if he is permanently disabled, this would be a restful place. With that thought, I took the leap of faith, and we bought the overpriced fixer-upper. It was way over our heads in cost, but I believed it would provide the right healing environment.

I worked like a dog, my usual coping strategy for dealing with stress, but it didn't matter. Like everyone else, I soon sensed the heat of the boss on my neck. Everything I turned in slightly missed her expectations. My co-workers were helpful and supportive, speaking in coded terms such as, "She's like that; she treats new people like a rookie in a newsroom."

Despite their reassurances, I believed I was failing. It didn't matter that one co-worker, Carrie, seemed to bear the boss' wrath daily, even worse than me. Although she had arrived before me and had years of experience like me, everything she submitted was slightly unacceptable.

By the end of the week, Carrie was fired and escorted from the building. Even though this was proof that the boss had a nasty habit of churning through staff, I could not believe it was happening to Carrie, much less that it could happen to me. She did nothing wrong. I knew because I worked beside her every day. When I asked the editor about it, she mumbled, "Watch out; the boss likes to fire people."

I froze. OMG. My stomach churned. I could be next. What about my husband? The house? I couldn't let my mind go there. She couldn't be that evil, right? I decided to work harder and meet her every demand.

Soon, I met Carrie's replacement, a vivacious woman who taught writing and rhetoric classes at a prestigious college. We immediately connected, and I thought we could overcome any issue with the devil boss.

That was short-lived. Predictably, with Carrie gone, the devil came for me. She needed a new employee to hold up to the team as inadequate.

I pressed the editor for answers. What's up with her? This office? That is when the editor said the devil "has fired three previous staff members." I let out an audible gasp.

All that time, I still thought it was me. I'm not good enough. I had to get better. Even with my new coworker reminding me that my work was fine and something else was afoot, I sensed inadequacy and unworthiness somehow. I assumed that bosses know best. I don't know, but for some reason, I felt responsible for the boss' unhappiness, which was a notion I could not shake.

With my back against the wall, I contacted everyone in my D.C. network that night. "There's been a change of plans; I am back on the market. Do you know anyone who is hiring?" It was short and sweet but urgent. Underneath it all, I was melting. As possibly the sole provider in the future, I knew I had to get another job fast, and desperation set in.

The next day, I got a message that the devil had scheduled a meeting with the human resources lady and me for later in the week. The devil had allowed my hours to increase to full-time, but she had some questions she wanted to discuss among the three of us. My hands shook. I was cornered. Even though my work was acceptable, it did not matter. What mattered at this moment was the petty power of a tyrant who could wreck my family life and my future career.

By then, we had moved into the Cape Cod, but the living room was still filled with moving boxes. I remember that day vividly. I let myself in, absorbed the quiet of the house, and dropped to my knees on the hardwood floor. "Please, God, help me," was all I could muster. I stayed there for a while, watching the dust settle in the sunlight.

There's a certain freedom when you hit the end of the worry chain like that. Despite my rusty prayer technique, my burden lifted, and I sensed a little shift inside. It's like I worked through the worst-case scenario in my head and heart and found I was still breathing. What a pleasant surprise. Hope trickled back in.

The very next day, a previous US State Department friend called me to say they had an open media affairs job. I jumped in a taxi to speak with the hiring manager in person. She asked about my availability. I looked her in the eye and slowly said, "Immediately."

She registered my pain and said, "It sounds like a bad fit." My insecurity bubbled to the surface. Was I the bad fit? "No," she said, "it means the right person is in the wrong job." I sighed in relief while she instructed her assistant to hire me on the spot. I blinked in disbelief. My prayer had been answered.

The highlight was telling the devil and the HR lady that I could not make their meeting because I was transferring to another agency. They reacted like two criminals caught in the act: throat clearing, hemming, hawing. I could see embarrassment in the HR manager's face. She knew this was the devil's way and was powerless to change it. Averting my eyes, she said weakly, "Ah, congratulations; we'll get that paperwork together for you."

In today's world, an employee assistance program would probably be in place if I chose to challenge them for creating such a toxic work environment. Back then, though, I was grateful to avoid such a close call with a stopped paycheck.

I was not empowered to confront the bully boss before finding a new job. My insecurities, immediate financial worries, and perception that I had no choice made that impossible. It spooked me for life. From that day forward, I learned to be my advocate and brand, armed and ready to defend my work and reputation at any moment.

As a best practice, I keep a current portfolio of my work and my references ready on my website. I also maintain open accounts on job search engines and stay up-to-date on the trending hiring needs within my industry. This situational awareness is empowering: I know my value in the marketplace and the current opportunities at any given time.

Call it my security (or insecurity?) blanket, but this practice shifted my focus from external boss-pleasing to internal brand management, improving my confidence and independence.

I advise friends to create a list of tough questions when researching a future employer, such as: What is the biggest obstacle to this job? What support will you provide to overcome that obstacle? How do you resolve conflict in your organization?

The questions let the hiring manager know the candidate is interviewing them as much as they are being interviewed, and the answers to these questions speak volumes about the manager and the organization.

I vowed never to let another boss hold my future in their hands.

your turn...

Claim your power

Do you believe you deserve better but are afraid to advocate for yourself? Take a minute to remember you are more powerful than you think. Then, write down your answers to these questions:

Where are you giving away your power? Is what you are getting in return worth it?

What inner beliefs do you hold about your power as an employee? How do they serve you? What do you believe is at risk if you claimed your power and advocated for more of what you need to thrive at work?

Do you have a current work portfolio and references ready to position yourself for a sudden change in your work situation? If not, how can you create them? How will this allow you to operate from a place of confidence instead of fear?

Kathleen Goggin

RULE 3
Go Lateral

Starting a new job from a desperate place is never a good thing.

Immensely grateful that I had narrowly escaped the devil woman's wrath, I was pressured to begin the next job immediately and keep my paychecks flowing.

My husband's illness seemed endless. He took as much sick leave as possible, and daily activities were challenging. This thought constantly plagued me: "What if he has to be on disability?" The pressure of a mortgage with his uncertain health kept me up at night. We had a 7-year-old at home, and I felt the entire weight of the world crushing down on me.

In this state of fear, I started the challenging media affairs job. I was part of a two-person team answering media questions mostly about distressed Americans overseas, covering all geographic areas of the world in all time zones.

The urgent stories were about the sad things that can happen to US citizens abroad: arrests, deaths, kidnappings, and evacuations. We also responded to inquiries about everything from visas to passports to student travel. I believed I was on the right side of the media machine this time, writing for the public good; still, the work volume and pace were staggering.

Then, suddenly something was off in the passport production office. Brides missed their destination weddings and students couldn't depart because their passports weren't delivered in time for travel. In meetings, brides were blamed as irresponsible or unaware. This struck me as downright odd. I have never met a bride who was not all over every single detail of her destination wedding. As the leaves began to turn color that fall, my gut said something was very, very wrong in the passport office.

Soon, the media started investigating, and information began to seep out. Yes, there were production delays at the manufacturing level. Yes, there were longer lines at passport centers. Yes, there was a growing backlog. People were getting more and more anxious about their travel plans.

Then, just after Christmas, the shit squarely hit the fan. A little-known regulation went into force on Jan 1, 2007, New Year's Day. The US Department of Homeland Security (DHS) would now recognize "border crossing cards." Huh? What was that? How was that different than a passport?

DHS had not coordinated well with the State Department; if they did, it had not trickled down to our office. The whole country was suddenly confused on day two of the new year. With the existing passport production delays and this new travel document, the stage was set for a head-on disaster ... and panic set in nationally.

We were soon overrun with hundreds of media calls and juggled late-night and weekend coverage. Although our office had other staff who were not busy, we struggled to get their help. I realized with a sinking feeling that no reinforcements were coming.

My husband was still recovering. His employer was accommodating and understanding, but each day was a struggle. He did not talk about his illness and worried about how it would affect his career options. He was a responsible, hard-working person who was pressured to provide despite his limited abilities.

I was equally challenged. Frazzled by the crisis at work and my overwhelming responsibilities at home, I operated in a constant state of anxiety. Once an avid cook, my husband tried to help, but could only make a can of soup before lying down exhausted. The debilitating head pain, short-term memory loss, and other symptoms had not been resolved since that fateful event the previous July.

Then, one day, I came home to an unlocked front door and a gas burner flaming on the stove. My husband had forgotten both. My heart stopped, and I folded in two, grabbing my knees. That was my literal breaking point.

I called in sick the next day. Recently, I had heard of a "lateral" job with regular hours at the training center closer to home. A lateral meant I could make the same salary. Since onward and upward pay increases are a marker for career success, I had to weigh this type of job and the long-term implications of my career ladder climb.

As I updated my resume for the second time in nine months, I knew changing jobs would make me look like a job hopper, the dreaded designation my mother told me I should never be. By the end of the day, I knew I could not continue working in an understaffed crisis situation with my competing home life needs.

A friend who was a writer/editor at the training center held the lateral job. She was leaving for a non-profit position and enthusiastically recommended me to her top-notch manager. I qualified for the job and had my portfolio and references in order. They were pleased to find a great candidate to bridge their pending office gap. It was finally the right fit at the right time.

I knew this lateral move would not be the job I retired from, but it was a healthy temporary structure that supported me during that difficult life phase. I had to explain later to potential employers why it appeared I took "a step back" in my upward trajectory, but I tackled this head-on with the truth. I figured if they couldn't understand the situation and my reaction to it, I didn't want to work for them.

Like a tree, it's okay to branch out laterally so your roots can become strong again. There is no shame in it.

It is also okay to not always be the star crew member rescuing the sinking ship. While it's important to be loyal to an organization, they also need to reciprocate. If not, a tipping point is reached when the price of loyalty is too high.

The training center position restored my work-life balance for a while. I knew all the changes that year wore out our family. The new job was a peaceful environment, and I found satisfaction in providing useful pre-deployment information to officers and staff on their way to overseas posts. The hours were perfect and allowed me to meet my son after school each day with a clear head.

That might not sound important to everyone, but it was huge to me at that critical time. As a working mom, I was always conflicted with time management. Being home for my son after school meant a lot to me, and I was more fulfilled as a working parent.

I always advise other parents, "Work, stay home, or do both if you want, but be the parent you want to be, then you can be the worker you want to be." Embracing that mantra for myself is how I finally found the right balance.

My husband finally started improving, and things settled down. During those years, I gave myself time to breathe, learn, and grow. I strengthened my resolve personally and professionally, preparing me well for future job transitions.

your turn...

Go lateral

I appreciated the media affairs job and thought I should follow through and show my loyalty to the manager who had saved me from the devil. But the reality of the situation cut through that idea daily. I knew I needed to work less and find more support for my whole life, not only my work life.

Do you feel like you should stay in a situation despite your glaring reality? Take some time for yourself today and find your answers to these questions:

Is it your voice you hear or an echo from your parents or community? Is this false loyalty keeping you anxious, afraid, and off-center?

What level of respect do you require from your bosses or management team? Have they missed the mark in how they treat you? Have you done your best to make what you expected clear?

What image or metaphor represents the restored balance or opportunity a lateral move might offer?

What beliefs or perspectives do you need to let go of to embrace the benefits of a lateral move during this season in your life or career?

RULE 4
Observe, Don't Absorb

We lived in the D.C. area for several years until my son was in middle school. During that time, I created and sold an iPhone app, Backpack Kids: The Safety Planning Checklist for Overseas Travel. This time, my passion project helped parents, teachers, and volunteer leaders plan international travel for school-age children.

I transitioned from the training center job to an engaging outreach position with a Western water agency. As a born and raised Easterner, my colleagues quickly educated me about natural resources management and the longstanding Western water wars.

During that job, I reported to a great manager who taught me the real power of editing. I valued the job, the people, and the purpose — and I also developed an interest in national parks since they usually bordered our dams.

Writing for national parks became a new goal, and I obtained a high-level certification to plan, write, and edit comprehensive communication plans for them. My ongoing daydream was to live and work in nature. I hoped to transition to that type of writing, but unfortunately, no park jobs were open then.

In 2012, as I approached my third year on the job, my husband was thinking about his next international assignment. Supporting his career meant I would need to quit my job again, yet honestly, at that point, with no promotion or park transfer options available, I could easily prioritize my husband's career over mine this time. I took a short break from working after he accepted a new posting to Mexico City.

We had a blast living in that warm and welcoming culture, but the US government ran out of money during his tour of duty in 2013. My husband was sent home from the office and told to stay put until Congress could fund the government. He kept busy completing DIY projects in our apartment, yet by the 16th day of waiting to return to work, he decided to plan his retirement.

This meant I would start my next job hunt early in 2014. I plugged into my network of former bosses and co-workers and heard about a contract position in D.C. It was an events office back at the State Department, primarily planning presidential summits or major meetings between world leaders.

This opportunity attracted me for several reasons. My dad died rather suddenly when I was young, and his work supported presidential summits. On some level, I wanted to feel connected to him and follow in his footsteps.

Even though I was gun-shy about tackling event management again, I rationalized it was a great option for the right price. Also, it was a limited-time contract, which gave me short-term money while searching for my next long-term position.

Since our house was rented and my husband and now 15-year-old son were still in Mexico, I lived temporarily with my nephew in Virginia during this job stint. It was a helpful setup until my family could be reunited in our home again.

I dove into work right away, assisting with the media plan for the first African-American Leaders Summit which took place later that year.

I adored my delightful young colleague, the project lead. It was my first-time reporting to someone in his 20s, and I swiftly got used to his creative talent and decision-making by text. He was brilliant and simply said, "Your job is to be me if I am hit by a bus."

I got it, loud and clear: I had no real job tasks of my own; I was only his back-up. That made me feel a bit underemployed, but I was fortunate to have this job. My friends and family recommended that I take it easy and do the bare minimum, but the "good girl" in me would not let me slack off. I found ways to be steadily productive despite the limited requirements.

The director, on the other hand, was cool and collected. She had a successful reputation building teams composed of political appointees, event experts, and a mix of recent retirees from different specialties. There were staff rumblings, though, that she wielded her power like a sword, could be a bitch, and practiced the "visual school of management."

That meant if a big project was pending, you might get assigned if you were the first person she saw after the kickoff meeting. Whereas some folks actively hid from the director, we got along well.

The big summit came and went. I was proud of my work for that historical event, but I was already eyeing the end of the contract and the next, more career-oriented position. More importantly, though, I focused on reuniting my family under one roof again.

Then, one day in April, I headed to my cubicle, and it happened. I passed the director in the hallway, and she said, "I need you in Kenya in June. Get your immunizations updated. We will travel immediately to start planning." This was a directive, not a question. I stammered, "Um, I will check with my family. We should be moving back into our house then." Her curt response? "Figure it out."

Clearly, she thought I would stay at this job longer. I delivered on every task I promised, so I understood she wanted me for another event, but we had never discussed my future plans.

Now, she was making a non-negotiable demand I did not want to fulfill. There was no way I would leave my family in the lurch. We were going to reunite at home in June.

Her tone stung me, but I was more confident and empowered now and knew I had options this time. If I kept my eyes on the prize, I could smoothly transition, hopefully with a positive reference in hand.

I was fortunate to find another contract job in another part of the department. I would avoid media affairs and instead write, edit, and collate briefing books for an incredible executive I had worked with previously. The key deciding factors were better pay, well-recommended co-workers, and no international travel.

My biggest concern was that the new job was narrowly related to my writing interests and seemed more administrative, but I rationalized that it was close enough.

Now, I could give my notice to the director.

The phone conversation was remarkable. Walking downtown to lunch, it stopped me in my tracks.

Me: Thank you for the opportunity to work in your office. I am giving you my two weeks' notice, and I will be working for an executive in another office.

Director (sneering): I knew you were unhappy.

Me: What?

I was floored by her tone and angry reaction.

Director (shouting): I knew you were unhappy.

Me: Um, what? I'm not sure what you are saying. I am giving my notice.

What did happiness have to do with it? And why was she so mad?

Director (contemptuously): I heard you. Do you know I sit next to that executive in high-level meetings?

Me: Uh, no.

Director: Yes, I do ... and I know her.

The implied threat was that she would ruin my reputation with my new boss as payback for leaving. I acutely felt her power sword plunge like an off-boarding side swipe.

Me: I know her too. She's great.

Director: Oh, you do, hum?

That seemed to shut her down.

At that moment, I deciphered that she expected some level of loyalty for this temporary job. That and her subsequent vitriol confused me.

I had to push it aside in my head. I was determined to depart in the most professional manner possible. I took the high road and hoped to salvage some connection.

Me: Thank you again for the opportunity. I will give the executive your regards.

Director (disgusted): Yeah, you do that.

And that was that. Thankfully, nothing came of her veiled or not-so-veiled threat.

I had dodged another bullet. I had no idea of the venom hiding in those high-heeled shoes.

Rather than waste time feeding her narcissism, I observed and did not absorb her actions. I was responsible to me, not everyone around me.

I also leaned on my excellent co-workers to get through the next two weeks. They were happy for me, and I found solace in their support.

I learned that you walk into an existing situation in every office and never know who awaits you, so don't sweat it. Your employer is human with a whole backstory you know nothing about. She might also have many personal projections about you and your role — all hidden. This is not your problem.

If I am ever in the position, I want to be the classy boss that departing employees praise and admire. I raise my glass to the graceful exit. Employees deserve and expect better.

your turn...

Observe, don't absorb

Some people will always take your actions personally, no matter how professional you try to be.

Are you now, or have you ever been, in a similar spot in your work? Take a moment and write down your answers to these questions:

Do you feel your boss has/had some untrue personal projections of you? List them here, and mindfully observe them. Do not absorb them.

In what past situations have you absorbed the emotions of your boss or colleagues? What can you learn from those experiences to support you now?

What habits or patterns do you recognize in yourself about using emotions as a currency to generate action? How motivated are you by others' emotional appeals?

What practices do you have in place (or want to create) to maintain your emotional stability and presence when overcome by emotions "in the moment"?

Kathleen Goggin

RULE 5
Align Interests & Skills

I reveled in my work for the executive in my old office. I was well qualified for the briefing book job because of my previous experience, and I was attracted to the lack of travel, regular hours, and writer/editor aspect.

The work content was straightforward, although the briefing book style guidelines were very quirky. Though iPads were in use, I printed the books on paper and assembled them manually into massive binders weighing six to seven pounds each. The big catch was I implemented this requirement with one faulty printer.

Some sections had to be printed one-sided, and some sections had to be printed double-sided. This immediately became a serious challenge because that unreliable printer was the only one that could print on both sides of the paper.

The books contained agendas, speeches, invite and participant lists, and trip schedules for multiple cities and sometimes multiple countries. A second backup book was also required for any staffer assisting with logistics during the trip. Since I collected data for each book from 50 to 100 people in headquarters and at overseas posts, I had to edit it into the proper style format. As time-consuming as that was, it did not compare to all the last-minute changes that required me to work late. Again, and again.

The sheer amount of time and effort that went into this old-fashioned production model was completely inefficient and under-calculated.

Mostly, I sat in a windowless corner working alone, cranking out these books. It went smoothly for a while, and I also produced briefing books for Congressional briefings. That was an enlightening experience and gave me new respect for the enormous amount of preparation that goes into those live presentations by government leaders.

One of the first signs the job was not sustainable long-term was the constant demand for late hours. This was not a reflection of my work speed; it reflected a gazillion last- minute changes and breakdowns of the sole, inadequate printer.

My patience with the technophobes was waning. After many late nights consistently delivering two six-pound briefing books, I found less and less satisfaction in this work.

I was also aware this was another understaffed and underfunded situation. If I had more resources, I would have created templates for each book section, automated the entire process, and presented it on an iPad or iPhone.

I learned that I could not ask for more staff or funding as a contractor. I was expected to go above and beyond the call to fulfill the task, no matter how inefficient the process was.

The turning point came at the end of a long week prepping books for a bi-lateral meeting, two international trips to countries with multi-city meetings, and a significant visit to Russia.

After hours, I assembled the Russia book. I was sort of talking to myself when I had an epiphany: "I really don't care about our relationship with Russia." That simple thought led to a complete inner dialogue, and I asked myself, "Then what topic do you care about?"

I pondered that in the following weeks. I also talked through my issues with friends and family, yet my trusty journaling practice helped me most.

I planned a low cost get-away to gather my thoughts. Some people might prefer a spa or fancy retreat. For me, a hotel in the Shenandoah Mountains with a hiking trail and indoor pool did the trick. I got quiet, re-centered, and restored my strength.

I journaled intensely that weekend, which helped me reflect on my thoughts and feelings about the situation. I knew I wanted work that had more impact, yet I was unsure how to find it.

So, I created a new method. In one column, I listed all the things I like to do, and in a second column, I listed all the things I am good at. Then, I linked the work I enjoyed and the work I was good at with a line connecting each item in each column. I evaluated the new list and asked myself, "Of these choices, now what do you actually want to do?"

Bingo. It was clear to me. I didn't care about our relationship with Russia because I did not care about international affairs. I had only fallen into that topic because of my husband's international career. I missed writing about nature and its management.

Additionally, I came to terms with the type of worker I had become. As someone who would always choose family over career, I had to accept the temporary nature of my choices. My "career" was a patchwork quilt of jobs.

That is why I was a pinball bouncing between jobs that fit my family's circumstances. That is also why everything kept changing and evolving. I finally made peace with my priorities.

My husband did not. He could not understand why I did not feel "fulfillment" at work. His career was very structured and provided him with a proven path; he failed to see that I supported his career and our family with my job-versus-career choices.

This friction between us lasted many years.

I applied my "what do you want, want are you willing to do, and what are you willing to sacrifice" framework to work options in the natural resource world. Forests, parks, oceans, and their conservation were the topics that sparked joy, though sadly, those jobs were not high paying. Ultimately, I decided I could sacrifice a small pay drop if needed to return to that more satisfying work.

I was thrilled to land an interview with a company supporting the National Oceanic and Atmospheric Administration (NOAA). I learned they do a lot more than report the weather.

The office I was interested in measured environmental damage from oil spills, pollution events, and shipwrecks. Wow, that kind of impact excited me.

I was on solid ground now and headed in the right direction.

your turn...

Align interests & skills

Give some thought to your current situation. Are your interests aligned with your skills and your passions?

On the next few pages, write down your thoughts and answers to these questions:

Are you good at work you don't enjoy? What is the state of your current work engagement?

If you could minimize certain tasks, what would you spend less time doing? What would you spend more time doing? How would your work look different? Is reallocating your tasks in your role possible without leaving your current job?

Can you create temporary, part-time, or volunteer options to help you bridge to a more satisfying job?

What are some of your "peak" professional experiences? What and who was present?

Consider and list as many of these "peak" experiences and factors as possible to excavate patterns of joy or fulfillment in work. What clues do you see to create fulfilling work in the future?

Kathleen Goggin

RULE 6
Leverage Boredom

My transition to a new topic went somewhat smoothly.

I took extended personal leave over the Christmas holiday to care for my son, who was having major surgery. While in the waiting room, I got an offer for the NOAA contract job. On the call, I told the HR manager where I was, and she said, "I will pray for you and your family." Her compassion touched me so much that I accepted the job on the spot.

She was even fine with a delayed start date while I cared for my son during his recovery.

This meant I could give my notice while on extended leave and never return to my previous job. One of my colleagues loves to tell this story: "Kate went to lunch and never came back."

I recognized management's empathy in my new job from day one. My company cared about me as an employee, and the federal client also was supportive. They both emphasized a healthy work-life balance that they implemented.

I thrived supporting NOAA. It was a career highlight to assist scientific teams that had worked on the Deepwater Horizon oil spill and other fascinating issues, too.

I was stunned to learn scientists can regrow coral after a ship crashes into a reef. It's true; it works like it would in a garden nursery, only it's underwater.

And pollution. After working in this job for several years, I learned that a large swath of the American coastline is dotted with permanent pollution sites. There went my dream of owning oceanfront property.

The work had the impact I wanted, and I treasured my coworkers. Though many had PhDs, they never flaunted their expertise, and they were all very easy-going people united by the same mission. This was a position I sincerely appreciated.

The job changed, though, when I no longer appeared challenged. I was dealing with the multi-layered bureaucracy pushing a research story through reviews. One expert after another slowly added their input until the story was approved.

When I loaded it onto our website, I felt relief rather than pride. This was a new feeling and indicated to me that the work was becoming less energizing. I had mastered the job, and this fast-forwarded me straight to boredom.

I realized I had been selling myself short by repeatedly taking similar jobs to accommodate my complex work/life puzzle. Yet, I could not imagine taking a higher position while juggling my personal life. From my viewpoint, I never saw the same work-life balance initiatives applied to management positions. I watched managers suffer.

I stayed in the job, hoping to get promoted, only to learn our small company size could not accommodate that.

I was restless, too. I've heard this is common for trailing spouses. The pattern of moving every two to three years gets into our DNA, so even when it's no longer required, we crave a change to feel progress.

One tactic I tried was to apply for a federal position. If selected, I would join the staff of my federal client, and I would no longer be a contractor. I applied because I believed in the mission, and I wanted to continue writing for a positive purpose, "writing for good," as Julia Cameron notes. I was also interested in the generous benefits package – pension, 401K, personal leave, and a commuting subsidy. These seemed like valuable assets compared to our limited company benefits.

Unfortunately, like many candidates, I only heard radio silence after submitting my federal application.

By now, my husband had healed as much as we could hope. The brain infection left him with a daily headache and short-term memory issues, yet he managed to continue working.

Additionally, my son had recovered from his surgery and was now researching colleges.

At this point, I had been building my career for more than ten years and knew I wanted a change. With university expenses looming, I needed more money and variety, and I was willing to leave the subject matter I cherished to achieve it.

I thought switching from science writing to technical writing would offer more profitable opportunities. This was a tricky time because I had a vague notion about changing my writing specialty, yet I wasn't sure how to approach the switch.

I felt a pull toward technical tasks. Maybe it was my recurring longing to connect to my dad. One of my happiest childhood memories was sitting at his elbow, watching him repair something — a light switch, a drywall hole, or a broken crab pot. We focused on problem-solving and the instant gratification of fixing things. This idea of satisfying technical work bubbled up for me regularly, but the execution of it seemed elusive.

One of the best things I did during this stretch was to take training after hours on my dime. It signaled that I was being proactive and more self-directed in my career choices.

I also believed I was loosening up a bit with my overwhelming sense of responsibility to everyone and everything. A helpful mentor reinforced this feeling.

She noted that I might have been sensing an early indicator of my pending empty nest phase, or it might have been the budding idea to treat work as a journey, not a destination. Either way, we agreed I was growing in a new way.

I always advise people they should learn something new if their job search is in neutral. Gaining a credential while reconsidering work is the most productive way to lay low when we are uncertain.

I took my own advice and thought deeply about my list of possible jobs and the course of study that led to them. I found a technical writing certification program, and it was the best online training I ever received. The program included a variety of exercises that I embraced. Each project tapped into that familiar goal of solving problems and the instant gratification of fixing things. I knew I was on my way to more satisfying work, and the new credential set me up for higher wages and more opportunities.

By leveraging my boredom and restlessness, and opening up to a learning and growth experience, I enjoyed the journey more than I thought I would.

your turn...

Leverage boredom

Are you ready for something more challenging?
On the next few pages, consider how you could
reframe your boredom and restlessness by
answering these questions:

If you are parked in neutral, what are three new
subjects that interest you?

Can you complete a class, workshop, or
credential in one of those areas?

What parts of yourself or personal interests did
you set aside or put on the back burner in a
previous phase of your professional journey?
Would revisiting them now reveal clues about
more engaging, skillful work?

What might be a unique juxtaposition of
seemingly unrelated skills and interests you
have developed?

Kathleen Goggin

Kathleen Goggin

RULE 7
Forgive Yourself the Unknown

Excited and armed with my new certification, I interviewed at different companies, yet I had no actual vetting process. I searched the usual online employee rating sites, but I assumed all companies operated the same way as the reliable one I worked for supporting NOAA.

I accepted my next job based on these criteria: a significant pay increase, a shorter commute, and an excellent assignment to work in a technical topic area.

During the interview, I noticed right away that the CEO asked me questions and then answered them himself instead of waiting for a reply. The program manager, by contrast, oozed professionalism and poise. Her questions were thoughtful and the information she provided proved she expertly knew the job, the federal client, and the agency.

They told me 99% of my work would be with the program manager, so I figured I could deal with the CEO for our limited interactions. Little did I know I was about to learn a hard lesson about poorly defined roles and responsibilities.

The company office presented a start-up culture. Foosball, pinball, Nerf guns, and ping pong were all acceptable activities. Though the noise was distracting, I liked my coworkers and the new client. This was the honeymoon period.

When I understood what the client wanted, I called a meeting to scope the work. I wanted to update the program manager and the CEO, but I also needed more details about the company's production resources.

One of the client's top tasks would be to script, videotape, edit, and produce a monthly video series for an executive.

I had experience performing all those tasks, and I outlined the project details and schedule for the CEO.

When I asked about a videographer and editor, I was surprised to hear the CEO say he was the videographer.

This seemed off base since I was told his expertise was in network computing. I trusted him despite my nagging intuition that this did not make sense.

Then, the CEO told me I should delay the video editor's kick-off meeting because the editor was extremely busy.

This seemed weird, too, but I believed the company resources must be in place. How else could they perform this work?

The first red flag surfaced when we were ready to videotape the executive. The CEO struggled with the camera set-up and seemed confused about basic three-point lighting.

Sweat trickled down my face after he forced the executive to re-tape the scene several times.

Back in the office, I viewed the footage. Improperly lit greenish images confirmed my worst fears. He was not a professional videographer.

I wasn't sure what to do with this information. After all, the CEO had promised the company could perform and deliver this work.

The second red flag came when I called and emailed the video editor, and he was never available to meet. Despite this roadblock, I put together a rough footage edit list anyhow. I wanted to keep the production schedule on track. I sent him the list via email and crossed my fingers.

Strangely, I heard from him on a Monday. He had edited the rough cut over the weekend. My mind was spinning in frustration. Why couldn't I meet with this co-worker during the week, and why did he work on weekends? Would they expect me to work on weekends, too?

After a lot of hide-and-seek and rescheduled meetings, I looked him up online. His profile stated he was working full-time for another agency. If this were true, that would explain his strange schedule and unavailability.

This scenario left me queasy. I could not confirm his activities; I only knew the more I asked questions about him, the more the CEO reassured me everything was fine. This seemed like a classic "gas light" situation: I was told one thing, but my reality was something else. I was confused and afraid about what to do next.

I was squeezed between the client — who expected high-quality video presentations — and the company, which overpromised a product they could not deliver.

In the communications field, your work product is your calling card. So now my work product was sub-standard and not my fault, yet I was prohibited from explaining why. I worried about my professional reputation, and panic crept in.

My past job mistakes triggered me, and I turned inward, questioning myself repeatedly. How did I not know? Did I ask the wrong questions in the interview? Should I have done some other research?

Feeling very deceived, my thoughts turned to serious doubts. How can I make a change now? It will make me look like a job hopper ... again! How can I fix this and recover?

At this point in my career, every time I had taken one step forward, it appeared I took two steps back. I guess this was the trial part of trial and error.

I talked to my family and friends about my self-doubt. They helped me see that during the interview, I could know only 50% of the information. The company knew the other 50%. No matter how much I researched, I could never know their culture until I was in it.

I made the best decision based on the information I had at the time. I needed to forgive myself for the unknown. It was not my fault.

I also sought support from coworkers to get their take on the situation. They agreed it was untenable and contributed to why my predecessor left. They summarized it as the mismatch between what the company thought it could provide and what it could actually deliver — an existing problem based on management weakness — and not a reflection on my judgment.

Thankfully, updating my resume again was not a big effort, except this time, I would break the cycle. I would not take a similar job and I would ensure the salary was more competitive.

Ironically, the universe aligned the stars instead, and I did not need to beat the pavement. Like Oprah says, "Luck is when preparation meets opportunity," and that's what I sensed when I got a call from the NOAA HR man out of the blue.

It was almost a year later, yet they still had my federal application in hand. They wanted to know if I was interested in returning to support endangered species conservation. I sort of squealed yes, and I was delighted to schedule an interview. Feeling relieved, I welcomed the chance to embrace a new challenge at a reasonable salary while reuniting with my old contacts.

What is the takeaway from this chapter of my work life? I learned you can check every online resource and background story about a company; in the end though, you will only see half of the picture. Every job acceptance is a risk, and you must forgive yourself for the unknown.

your turn...

Forgive yourself the unknown

Sometimes, taking a new job is like going on a blind date. You cannot know if it's a match unless you go.

We take a leap of faith with every job change ... and sometimes we land where we find ourselves disillusioned, undermined, or gaslit. On the next few pages, stand back and consider your answers to these questions:

In what ways does your job differ from what you were expecting when you accepted it? Can you get comfortable with the things that don't match your expectations?

How much time do you spend believing you should have known something more about a difficult situation you may be in? Is this taking up hours of your day or evenings?

What is the right amount of time to consciously indulge in feeling bad, and when is it time to refocus by forgiving yourself what you could not have known?

What helps you tune into insights or gut instincts about your situation or others you work with? When can you sense them most clearly? What gets in the way of these hits? What makes you second-guess yourself?

RULE 8
Rise Above the Noise

By this time, I thought I had checked all the boxes of my new rules. I gathered momentum by moving to true motivations, aligning interests, claiming power, leveraging boredom, and accepting risk, yet I found myself surprised in new ways by the conservation unit job.

While I heard encouraging stories about their important work and dedicated staff in the interview, I also received vague warnings from previous colleagues that my new office employed "difficult people" and they could be "challenging to work with." No one actively advised me to turn down the job, yet they cautioned me about an agency-wide groan in response to this group.

I accepted the information as part of the usual mixed opinions of any office because I also heard affirmative things about the group and its mission. They had accomplished a lot with little staff and funding, and their expertise was recognized worldwide.

I was overjoyed and enthusiastic about joining their team. With my son in college and my husband retired, I thought I could finally make my career a priority. I wanted it to be "my turn," so my family could support my work now.

I poured myself into the work. I hit the ground running, and there were people with projects waiting for me, lined up at my cubicle. I was trying to make a good impression and juggle the stress. Nonetheless, my FitBit recorded the daily toll this job quickly took on my health. An elevated heart rate and trouble sleeping were some of the first warning signs of issues.

When I circled back to my managers, I did not get the guidance I hoped for. They were inexperienced and consumed with people's problems. The staff was like a cast of characters in a Greek play. There were protagonists, antagonists, and a choir constantly commenting on the central actions of the office.

"Passionate" workers filled the combative office culture and constantly argued their positions in endless meetings with no firm result.

Though the org chart depicted a hierarchical management structure, the reality was that everyone was in charge, with equal authority to change a task or an approach, at any moment.

The whole scene created a noisy, chaotic atmosphere for me.

Added to the office culture was the controversial conservation topic: whales and endangered species. It seems everyone in the world has a personal opinion about whales and endangered species. Those opinions usually conflict with commercial fishing, recreational fishing, naval operations, tourism, oil, gas, wind energy development, and conservation programs.

The staff lived with daily stress that any minor update could blow up into a news item, a congressional inquiry, or a lawsuit. Burnout was high.

This awareness gave me better insight into the group's conflict history with other offices and why they were dubbed "reactionary." Yet even when insiders or outsiders went out of their way to be accommodating, this group found a way to undermine those efforts. It was as if the group had an underdog identity they didn't want to give up.

That perception permeated the office. In meeting after meeting, their implied viewpoint was, "If you are on our team, you should feel this way too."

But I didn't. I saw how much everyone bent over backward to work with this group, and I was surprised every day by how myopic they remained. Past grievances and complaints hindered their present expertise and impact.

Still, I stuck it out for several years for economic reasons. I was paying for my son's college and our old Cape Cod mortgage. I also enjoyed the fascinating projects and the top-notch communication professionals in our service area and within the agency. Their comradery kept me afloat during those years.

My patience shifted, though, after two consecutive incidents. The first was a scientist's simple retirement announcement that resulted in several emotional meetings, extra work and extended deadlines; ultimately, the project was cancelled. The second was when my manager asked me to write my own agency-level award nomination for a highly successful outreach project.

That is when I learned the importance of having a good laugh at a completely ridiculous work expectation. I knew I would never fit in with this group.

My plan had gone sideways again. I was disappointed and tired of being disappointed.

Maybe I had it all wrong about a straight career path. Maybe it was a long and winding road of self-discovery instead.

I did not need to be part of this office drama, and I could choose to spend my positive energy elsewhere. As I pondered that idea, I asked myself, "How have I contributed to the noise?" I knew myself better now and acknowledged my sensitivity and past experiences had also influenced my actions (and reactions).

I set out to learn more about my office personality and how it might affect others. I took the Myers-Briggs Personality Indicator test and the more reliable Gallup StrengthsFinder 2.0 test and concluded I was an introverted, organized, goal-oriented worker who appreciated a structured environment.

As my mentor emphasized, the solution would not require overthinking; a more disciplined office in the agency would be better for me.

I wished I could dial up my dad and ask for advice, but like everyone else, I turned to the Internet for help instead. I read the Harvard Business Review classic, "Who's Got the Monkey" (Oncken and Wass, 1999), about time management and delegation, and the famous "No Asshole Rule" (Sutton, R., 2007), about how negative individuals can ruin a team.

Both helped me understand I no longer wanted to be all things to all people in a confusing environment. Instead, I was interested in a promotion and more time spent with the top communicators in my agency.

I worked on projects with their staff frequently, and I got to know the exceptional manager there. Even though it would be a media-related position again, I believed it would be different this time.

I was secure knowing the manager and the office workflows. It appeared there was a cross-trained group, ready to provide back-up as needed. I was confident I would thrive on an inspiring team.

When the opportunity arose, I transferred to their office for a promotion.

I learned I could calm myself and rise above the noise to tolerate irritations and disappointments by knowing my work self better. This new resolve helped me be more strategic in my daily work life and my future jobs.

your turn...

Rise above the noise

Think back to a time when emotions got in the way of work. In the next few pages, consider your answers to the following questions:

What are the specific kinds of noise within your workplace? Are you still able to produce? What strategies have worked for you to tune it out ... or at least turn down the volume?

What kind of impact does this noise have on your body, your mental state, and your time away from the office?

What is your role in contributing to the noise? What can you do to redirect your energy?

What can you do to distance yourself and rise above the noise?

What is the cost of tolerating this noise?

Kathleen Goggin

Kathleen Goggin

RULE 9
Bet on Yourself

Have you heard the expression, "Find your people, then work with them"? I experienced this when I transferred to the agency communications team. These amazing professionals handled every possible communication situation with professionalism and seasoned expertise.

Believe me, that's not easy during normal times, much less during a global pandemic or a time of tumultuous political upheaval.

By achieving this promotion, I reached a career pinnacle, and I was honored to be on this new team. I was working for an excellent manager who was also an exceptional editor. I mean, next level.

He taught me so much about cutting jargon and clarifying tech talk that I could actually see the word count reduce and the readability score increase. Not only was he a great teacher, he was a wonderful person. We each brought a special ingredient to the team. I was fortunate to work there.

Our work filled headlines daily. Hurricanes, shark attacks, Right Whale conservation, illegal fishing, discovery of new species, and habitat restoration are a few that come to mind.

I often had to work weekends, which I was willing to do because the team shared the difficulty and the praise.

Still, there were only two of us again, and covering dozens of media inquiries daily was exhausting. The simultaneous stories about live animals were especially challenging and spanned every stage of their life cycle in every time zone. Imagine juggling monk seal or dolphin harassment in Hawaii, a sick baby Right Whale in Massachusetts, Mexican fishermen stealing high-value red snapper in Texas, and a 90,000-pound, gray whale dying on a public beach in California.

The upside included opportunities to fill in for my boss during vacations or absences. This experience revealed a view into management I had not seen before, and for the first time, I imagined myself as a future manager.

We were empty nesters now, and my husband was equally engaged in his post-retirement consultancy business. It seemed the right time to prepare myself for the next step up the career ladder.

I was thinking about these goals when I met with a professional coach in the fall of 2020. She reminded me that I was an incredibly conscientious worker with a long track record of high performance and success. She offered one insight that resonated with me: "You only feel successful externally; it's time for you to feel successful internally too."

She was right. My coach helped me identify my limiting beliefs and how my fear and previous experiences were holding me back.

I was still journaling daily when a new goal popped up: more independence. That might have been related to my growing interest in starting my own consultancy business and working remotely. I was unsure what form independence might take, even while I recognized its truth.

During this time, I also signed up for a Mission Collaborative Bootcamp offered through my college alumni association. Unlike most career planning retreats, this one opened my eyes to a bigger vision of my work life and the power of my network. It reminded me of my deeper motivations to write useful information to help people. I was also introduced to a new community of professionals who became a valuable sounding board for my business plan and proposed projects.

Meanwhile my job was evolving as they always do. My great manager left for a well-deserved promotion, which meant I was doing his job and mine while scrambling to find temporary help. This continued for several months, yet I was not compensated for the higher-level work. That left an impression on me and influenced my thoughts about future work with this organization.

As part of the bootcamp follow-up, I wanted to learn about independent consulting. I contacted a former coworker who owned a small communications company. I was familiar with their client and the technical topics covered, and I hoped to get an informational interview with her.

Instead, she was thrilled to hear from me because one of her clients had just identified a new need for a consultant. Was I interested? Absolutely.

While I had mixed feelings about leaving NOAA and the communications team I valued, the timing was right. I was trading the security of an agency job in exchange for the independence I craved.

I sensed I was done waiting in line to get recognized within an organization, and I'd rather bill for my services instead. I realized the management position I wanted was my own.

I learned it's okay to bet on yourself, even if unsure where your journey may lead.

Kathleen Goggin

your turn...

Bet on yourself

Independence comes in many forms, and you don't have to start a business to feel it. However, you do need to build your success from the inside.

On the next few pages, take a moment to reflect on your answers to these questions:

If you can have everything, but not at the same time, what continues to be a low priority? What does that tell you? What is your consistent top priority? Are you aligned with your answers?

How would you define success for yourself?

Which of your qualities, characteristics, skills, habits, or mindsets gives you the confidence to bet on yourself?

What past experiences do you need to review to excavate learning and update an outdated story you've been telling yourself?

What experiences or achievements would you pursue if you set fears aside and bet on yourself?

Kathleen Goggin

Kathleen Goggin

RULE 10
Embrace Uncertainty

Updating my resume for consultant work was a revelation. To justify my daily rate, the client did not want a summary of my experience; they wanted documentation of every communications job I ever had. Talk about journaling!

Hard work, credentials, awards, recommendations — it was all there and easily justified my day rate and also reinforced my inner sense of success. Finally, all of these jobs were adding up and leading to more satisfaction.

I brought all that experience to help my new client. I loved working with them, and they sincerely appreciated working with me.

Consulting was the perfect mix for several years. I tapped back into the fun of technical writing and the instant gratification of fixing text. I enjoyed a long stretch of meaningful work where my writing truly had a positive impact.

I also continued my personal development activities. I was getting older and interested in reinvention. My entire view of work had morphed, and I wanted to test myself in a new way, yet I was uncertain about what form that would take.

I kept returning to my interest in writing as perhaps a more creative outlet.

When I was young, I was not what you would call a reader. I was more interested in playing sports than curling up with a book. Yet at this later phase of life, I discovered the treasures in my local library.

I started reading more fiction, plays and poems. I studied writers I admire, such as Anne Lamott, Alice Walker, Cheryl Strayed, Maya Angelou, Tayari Jones, Tyler Perry, and Walter Mosley. I watched interviews with them and analyzed their work.

I love to learn, and fortunately, I found the work of Peter Elbow online (Kanopy, 2019). His presentations changed my whole attitude about writing. He taught me to make a mess and talk to myself on paper. This permission to let go of perfection and enjoy the writing experience was exactly the right formula to follow.

I was well aware that writing is manual labor. There is no substitute for the work and time in the chair. I increasingly wondered if I would feel differently about the writing profession if I didn't devote all my time and energy toward client projects. A central question emerged for me: What if I applied my knowledge, skills, and abilities toward creative writing projects I really cared about?

I knew that would be a huge risk. No one quits their day job while hoping for a publishing deal. Yet, with new, serious health problems for myself and my husband, I found I cared less and less about my day job, and I valued my creative time more and more.

I considered this value shift and met with a financial planner to figure out how to live frugally on my limited pension and our joint savings.

I also researched storytelling techniques. One lesson, an interview with Jill Chamberlain (Film Courage, 2020) stuck with me. She said that to keep an audience or reader interested, your story must involve some character transformation.

"If it doesn't, you have a situation, not a story," she said.

I realized I had lost interest in retelling my work-life situations to myself and others. I had not transformed, and it was time for me to confront that.

To address my security needs, I made more drastic financial decisions. My son had graduated from college and I was done with those expenses, so we downsized our house to reduce further expenses. Fortunately, my husband carried me on his health insurance and his pension and part-time income would stretch much further in our new hometown.

As part of my transformation, I also wanted to build a new community, one that was not office-based but instead focused on shared writing interests. I attended a few writers' conferences, and I was overwhelmed by the warm welcome I received. I was feeling more and more like I had found my people again in a new way.

One day after house-hunting, I stopped into a local bookshop for an author signing event. I met Beverly, the friendly owner, who was also a published writer. She put me on the mailing list, and I was happy to join her community for journaling workshops and author talks. Soon, she introduced me to Carol, her publisher and the heart and soul behind the 10 Little Rules book series.

I always imagined authors in dusty little rooms, secluded from daily life. Yet with each event, I met authors in every genre, and they were like me, usually working a day job while planning a writing project at night.

Then, in the fall of 2021, I attended the bookstore anniversary party. I met several writers including Kelly, a fiction writer, and Wendy, another 10 Little Rules writer for Carol's book series. I was dizzy with inspiration when a woman approached me from across the room.

"Kate Goggin. You probably don't remember me, but we worked together more than 20 years ago at the National Press Club," she said, with a lovely smile.

Oh my god, what were the chances? My treasured NPC colleague, Leigh Ann, lived in my new town, and the bookstore owner was her dear friend. I had goosebumps. This was a sign I had come full circle.

I also sensed an identity shift. I started to see myself as an independent writer, not just a technical writer or consultant. I was attracted to the freedom of writing for myself, and I was excited by the endless possibilities.

I figured I could continue a few small technical writing contracts while I pursued more creative projects. I wondered, what if I went all in, embraced uncertainty, and let go of my fears?

As I compiled my retirement paperwork, I texted "the hive," our bookstore writer community.

"I am doubled over laughing as I look at my career list," I texted. While I worked with mostly amazing people, I encountered a cast of characters, and I survived a lot of good jobs that went bad.

One friend joked, yes, you should create 10 Little Rules to Survive Bad Jobs. Then Carol, the publisher, immediately responded.

"Seriously, Kate, what about it? Want to really write that book?"

Stunned, I said, absolutely, I could write that! She drew up a contract and my next career chapter emerged.

There was no job interview or application, and we had never worked together before. Yet, we liked each other's work, and that gave us instant respect and trust. Added to those factors, we knew each other well. That day felt like we held hands and dove off a cliff together, pure magic.

During the writing process, I came to terms with the career narrative I had told myself over the years. I confirmed my character had changed through this story, and of course, the title changed several times because of it.

Throughout my career, I have counseled and mentored so many people by sharing my experiences; I hoped that by publishing this book, I could help even more people.

I tried to juggle my day job and book writing for a while, but eventually, I was comfortable with my financial situation, flipping my priorities and committing to full-time personal writing while continuing with part-time technical writing. Tipping the scales this way has brought me immense joy despite the uncertainty.

Of course, not all my jobs had been bad, and even the ones that went sour had all started out well. Sometimes the change came from the organization, sometimes from me, but in the end, I finally embraced the changes inherent in any career and fixed my work and my life.

Kathleen Goggin

your turn...

Embrace uncertainty

What stories are you telling yourself about what needs to be true so you can embrace uncertainty? Can you edit your list of "must haves" to accommodate greater acceptance of the uncertainty inherent in your career pursuits?

What can you stabilize in your personal life so that you can embrace uncertainty in your career?

What rewards or outcomes make embracing uncertainty worth it to you?

What would your life look like if you went all in on that dream job or project?

Kathleen Goggin

Kathleen Goggin

EPILOGUE

You know the expression, "You have to forgive your parents, otherwise you'll stay a child?" I think there is a version of that in the work world, too: "Forgive your bosses and your organization; otherwise, you'll stay child-like without satisfaction."

Our satisfaction is proportional to our self-knowledge, compassion, and expectations. Increasing those three things seemed to be the most important thing I learned.

I came to understand we bring our whole selves to the office; the nose-to-the-grindstone persona, as well as the insecure self, full of trepidation about whether or not we identify with our work, how it's done, and who we do it with.

I wish I could return to several jobs based on what I know now. If I could counsel my younger self, I would say, the only constant is change; it's all going to be okay and focus more on your own personal development instead of external motivators.

I would also reread William Bridges' book, "Transitions: Making Sense of Life's Changes." That foundation would have saved me a lot of work and life misunderstandings (Bridges, 2019).

If it's Sunday night and you are dreading Monday, you are not alone. The 2024 Gallup State of the Global Workplace report says, "The majority of the world's employees continue to struggle at work and in life, with direct consequences for organizational productivity." (Gallup, 2024)

Before you make a change, consider all your responses to each chapter. Take the time to reflect on the best choices for you first.

Every job is an important stepping stone to who you are and who you will become.

your turn, your rules...

Kathleen Goggin

158

Kathleen Goggin

Kathleen Goggin

Kathleen Goggin

References

Pryce-Jones, Jessica. (2010). Happiness at Work: Maximizing Your Psychological Capital for Success. Wiley.

Cameron, Julia. (2002). The Artist's Way: A Spiritual Path to Higher Creativity. J.P. Tarcher/Putnam.

Walker, Alice. (2002). Gathering Blossoms Under Fire: The Journals of Alice Walker, 1965–2000. Simon & Schuster.

Hull, Dana. (1998). Bonding Over the Expatriate Experience, Local Newsletter Supports Americans Living Overseas. The Washington Post.
https://www.washingtonpost.com/archive/local/1998/04/25/bonding-over-the-expatriate-experience/e172e058-0ed9-466b-aaea-933020dc5eeb/

Goggin, Kate. (2010). Backpack Kids: The Safety Planning Checklist for Overseas Travel. PR Newswire.
https://www.prnewswire.com/news-releases/recent-earthquakes-draw-attention-to-travel-safety-planning-for-kids-86260507.html

Certified Interpretive Planner (CIP) credential, National Association for Interpretation.
https://www.interpnet.com/interp/nai/_prof_development/cip.aspx?hkey=d34573b3-c4d2-447e-a18c-85640bea62ea

Certified Technical Writer credential, Ed2go.
https://www.ed2go.com/courses/writing/writing-and-editing/
ctp/certified-technical-writer

Haslam, S. Alexander. (2018). The Self-made Women Who
Created the Myers-Briggs. Nature.
https://www.nature.com/articles/d41586-018-06614-8

MBTI Online (2024) The Myers-Briggs Company.
https://www.mbtionline.com

CliftonStrengths Assessment (nee StrengthsFinder 2.0).
Accessed July 2024. CliftonStrenghts.com

Oncken, William Jr. and Wass, Donald L. (1999) Who's Got the
Monkey? Harvard Business Review.
https://hbr.org/1999/11/management-time-whos-got-the-
monkey.

About the Author

Writer, editor and author Kate Goggin has always been interested in sharing best practices in business and in life. Disappointed there were no manuals to follow, she often created those for herself, and then shared them to help others. "10 Little Rules When Good Jobs Go Bad" is her latest project, and is for anyone facing difficult decisions in their job journey.

A former "Family Matters" newspaper columnist, Kate has also published "The Art of International Living," a newsletter for successful overseas relocation, and "Backpack Kids: The Planning Safety Checklist for Overseas Travel," an iPhone app for parents, teachers, and volunteer leaders planning international travel for school-age children.

She is a certified technical writer and a former spokesperson. Her former clients include the US State Department, the National Oceanic and Atmospheric Administration, and the Federal Aviation Administration. She lives in Leesburg, VA.

Stay connected to the
10 Little Rules community
@10littlerules

Facebook
LinkedIn
Instagram

Watch for more 10 Little Rules books
launching soon
www.10littlerules.com